Soft Step & Bright Eyes

HAPPY READING!

This book is especially for:

Author Suzanne Tate
and
Illustrator James Melvin

Soft Step & Bright Eyes

A Tale of Native American Life

Suzanne Tate

Illustrated by James Melvin

Nags Head Art

Number 4 of Suzanne Tate's History Series

To Cora Mae Basnight
who warmed the hearts of many

Library of Congress Control Number 2001130043
ISBN 978-1-878405-32-6
ISBN 1-878405-32-2
Published by
Nags Head Art, Inc., P.O. Box 2149, Manteo, NC 27954

Printed in the United States of America

Soft Step and his little sister Bright Eyes were Native American children.

They lived a long time ago with their family on the sandy shore of Mosquito Bay. Other families lived nearby.

Mosquito Bay was a sparkling body of water. Native Americans often sat beside the bay, eating juicy meat from oysters.

The shells piled up—one by one —and made big hills.

The native families also ate fish and deer meat. Soft Step was a young boy, but he knew how to look for wild animals.

He had a soft step when he went looking for animal tracks.

One day, Soft Step sat down near a path
where he saw some tracks.
He hoped to see a tail popping up—
the white tail of a deer.

Bright Eyes came along and asked to join him. "If you stay here, you must be very quiet," Soft Step told her.

He was patient with his little sister and tried to teach her about animals.

“A deer has a great sense of smell,” Soft Step said. “And it’s nervous when it wags its tail!”

Soft Step and Bright Eyes sat quietly, barely breathing.

Suddenly, there was a buck—a male deer with a big rack of horns—standing right beside them! Its tail was wagging.

The big buck stomped its front feet! Bright Eyes wiggled a little, and a twig snapped beneath her.

The deer was scared and off in a flash— its tail waving like a white flag.

Soft Step began to scold Bright Eyes.
"You have caused a big buck to run away."
"I didn't mean to," the little girl cried.
"When I saw him, I was scared!"

"Oh, that's all right," her brother said.
He was sorry he spoke sharply to Bright Eyes.
"Let's go tell our father that we saw
a big buck nearby."

Their father was interested to hear about the deer. “But your mother is cooking the fish I caught,” he said. “We have plenty of food for now.”

The children could see the fish broiling over an open fire.

Bright Eyes and Soft Step liked to eat the fish—
they were always so fresh and sweet.
Their father worked hard to catch them
in Mosquito Bay.

The children's mother often cooked in a big clay pot with a round bottom. She cooked all kinds of food in the pot—meats and roots and nuts.

The family ate potatoes, corn and beans that they raised in a garden.
Soft Step and Bright Eyes helped their parents raise the vegetables.

Children were always helpful even if they were very young.
"Help me pound these nuts for bread,"
Bright Eyes' mother said to her.

The little girl took a stone in hand.
She pounded nuts in a larger stone
that was like a flat bowl.

Her mother mixed the nut meat with water
to make a mushy dough.
It made a soft bread when it was cooked.

The Native American family sat down on a woven mat to eat their meal. They didn't eat at a table.

Bright Eyes and her mother sat on one side, and her brother and father were on the other side. Wooden bowls of food were between them.

But Bright Eyes didn't eat much food that day
because she was not feeling well.
The little girl's eyes looked cloudy and dim.
And she became hot and filled with fever.

When dusk came, Bright Eyes lay down on a mat that was on the floor of her house.

Her mother was worried about her. “I’ll fix you some tea from the wild cherry tree,” she said. “Grandmother always says that will stop a fever.”

Bright Eyes drank the tea from a gourd
and lay still on her mat.
When morning came, the fever was gone,
and her eyes were bright again!

she called, "I feel fine now."

Her mother was happy and gave Bright Eyes a big hug.
Soft Step was glad that his sister was well too.
But he wanted to look for deer again.

"I am going to look for that big buck,"
he told his mother.
And he went off to search for deer.

He was surprised to find some strange new tracks on the shore of Mosquito Bay. They were different from any he'd ever seen before.

Soft Step didn't know that he had found the boot tracks of explorers from far across the sea! "I must tell my father about this," he thought. And he went right away to find him.

Soft Step's father was puzzled and hurried with him to the shore of Mosquito Bay.

They were amazed to see a large sailboat! Strange-looking men were rowing a boat nearby.

The men pulled up their boat and came ashore. They made friendly signs with their hands.

Later that day, the Native American father invited them to come to his house.

He showed the visitors strings of pearls that came from the oysters of Mosquito Bay.
The explorers then exchanged shiny metal knives for the pretty pearls.

Bright Eyes helped her mother prepare a fine meal. They laid out deer meat, many kinds of fish, corn and fruits.

The explorers enjoyed the native food and ate their fill. Then, they left and went away in their boat.

Soft Step and Bright Eyes watched them go.
"Are those men real people?" the little girl asked.
"Let's ask our father," Soft Step replied.

Their father answered wisely:
"Those men eat and sleep like we do.
They are only humans!"

Soft Step smiled. "I didn't track strange animals after all," he thought. "Will we ever see them again?" Bright Eyes wondered out loud.

"I don't know," Soft Step replied. "But I'm sure we will always remember when strange visitors sailed into our lives!"